LIFE IN
The 1950s

Mike Brown

The Home

The Second World War left Britain with huge debts which meant little to spend on luxuries. By the early 1950s the end of the tunnel seemed a long way off, yet a new age was on the way. The latest streamlined jet aircraft design had seized the public's imagination. The ideas behind it became the essence of fashionable design of everything from cars to furniture, so much so that the 50s became known as the jet age.

Fashionable furniture was low-slung – it was the age of the coffee table. Less was more in terms of decoration; legs were plain, rectangular or circular in section and tapering elegantly to the base. Shapes might be cuboidal, but were more commonly streamlined, flared, tapered or triangular, but with the corners rounded.

The most common material was wood, usually of a medium to light coloured grain, or with a section painted in a primary colour, or stark black or white. Upholstery was plain, often in primary or pastel shades. Alternatively, metal furniture, made from plain steel rod or chromed tubing, might be used in kitchens for chairs, tall stools and tables, with primary-coloured plastic-covered seats or surfaces.

Plain painted walls might finish the look, but this went too far for most. Wallpaper was the norm, usually in pastel shades. Designs might feature flowers drawn in a very primitive,

cartoon-like style, or food items, such as fish or fruit, for kitchens, and spacemen and rockets, horses or cowboys for children's rooms. Another popular style looked like tiles, brickwork, or rough stonework.

Developments in materials meant that skilled tradesmen were no longer required; do-it-yourself was a growing trend, and for most people DIY meant Barry Bucknell, whose BBC shows demonstrated how to update older properties, covering panelled doors with sheets of plywood and boxing in Victorian fireplaces.

As with any age, most people did not go to extremes; the larger items of furniture were usually somewhat subdued in style, up-to-date

◄ A combined sideboard and table, 1950.

The Sussex bungalow, the living room, 1959.

A dining-sitting room, 1952.

A modern kitchen unit which can be used as a table, 1951.

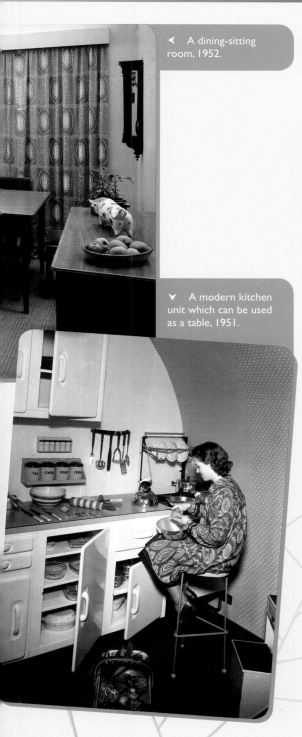

fashions being represented in smaller items, such as lamps or shades, magazine racks, radios, crockery or glassware.

Huge, chunky glass ashtrays, vases and jugs, in deep purples, blues, reds and oranges, were common, as were sets of drinking glasses, often hand-painted or transfer-printed showing exotic dancers or scenes from the South Sea Islands, Italy or Spain. Each set would have its own matching decanter or jug. Wall and ceiling lights took on an alien appearance with glass shades looking like gourds, while crockery designs in pastel or primary colours incorporated simple cartoon-type drawings, such as the Homemaker range.

Coffee or occasional tables with a base made of thin metal bars, often chromed or black with a glass top, or made from wood but using the framework design which looked more industrial than domestic, could be matched with table and chairs, or a magazine rack or candlestick. Manufacturers began to offer furniture ranges, so that pieces could be saved up for and a matching set built up. The most well-known example was G-Plan furniture, which first appeared in 1953.

Working Lives

The Blitz meant that there was a huge amount of rebuilding to be done. Unemployment remained low throughout the decade: in 1950 it was around 1.6 per cent, and by 1959 it was 2.3 per cent; the highest it reached was 2.6 per cent. This does not, however, take into account that far fewer women registered for work: under half, compared with about two-thirds today.

With such low unemployment, people could be choosy about which jobs they took, which led to labour shortages in certain low-paid professions, such as nursing and public

➤ A coalman delivering coke on a London street, 1959.

▼ Workmen put together a Ford Prefect on the final assembly line at the Ford Motor Works, 1950.

transport. The Government encouraged immigration from Britain's overseas colonies in the Caribbean, South Asia and Africa to fill the vacancies.

In the early 1950s, nearly 9 million people worked in manufacturing; between 40 and 50 per cent of the workforce. Today that figure is around 8 per cent. The UK was the second largest manufacturer at this time and the largest exporter of cars in the world. By 1960 it had dropped to third place in manufacturing; today it is in fourteenth place.

In 1950 there were 690,000 coal miners. This figure remained fairly stable until 1958, when it started to fall; by 1960 there were about 610,000 (today there are less than 10,000). In 1950 12 per cent of the workforce was described as managerial or professional; today that figure is 52 per cent. Interestingly, the number of public sector workers has remained roughly stable at 6 million, but as the size of the workforce has risen, as a proportion this figure has fallen.

Office work was far less automated; it was not until 1955 that the first automated copying machine came into being, and three years after that the first commercial push-button photocopier machine appeared. Without this typists had to make several copies of a document using carbon paper – a messy process. The computer was in its infancy; the world's first commercially available computer was the Ferranti Mark I, which appeared in February 1951. The first computer to undertake

▲   Apprentice bricklayers training in 1957.

business data processing appeared soon after, using electro-mechanical punched-card equipment. British firms were at the forefront of computer design, including Elliott Brothers, English Electric, Ferranti, and Leo Computers.

The school leaving age was 15; as today, final exams – then called Ordinary Level General Certificates of Education, or O levels – were normally taken at 16. Those leaving school early – which was the majority of pupils – would have no formal qualifications. Those entering skilled trades such as engineering, electronics or plumbing usually did so as apprentices. This was a type of on-the-job training. Apprentices would sign up, normally for three years, and by the end of their training they would be fully qualified. At first their wages would be very low, but their pay would increase to full rates by the time they successfully completed the training period.

In 1950 the average weekly wage was about £7 5s 6d (£7.28); adjusted for inflation that was about £211 a week. The average working week was around 44 hours, and the average holiday was 16 days a year. This might explain why Trades Union membership was 9.5 million, as opposed to 6.5 million today.

◄   The UNIVAC Super computer, 1956.

A t the start of the 1950s, Britain was still emerging from wartime austerity and food was still rationed. In May 1950, the points rationing system ended; in October 1952 tea came off ration; a year later it was the turn of sugar, followed in May 1954 by cheese, cooking fat and butter. In July bacon and meat became the last items to be taken off ration. After 14 years rationing was dead.

In the shops people queued up and gave their order to the shop assistant, who fetched the purchases. Far more goods were sold loose and were weighed out to individual requirements. However, in 1950 Sainsbury's opened a self-service store in Croydon. The concept was not immediately popular; people enjoyed the idea of being served, and much more food was pre-wrapped so you had to take the amount that was on offer.

There were far more small shops in the 1950s; the lack of freezers and often fridges in most homes meant that food was bought daily and prepared from scratch. This entailed daily trips to the butcher or fishmonger, baker and grocer. The Co-op accounted for about a third of the UK grocery market, usually in the form of small, local shops. In America, ready-prepared meals in the form of the frozen 'TV dinner' were being developed, but they required a freezer. In Britain the frozen fish finger was first produced by Birds Eye in 1955, but most people cooked them on the day they bought them.

There were department stores, the leading ones being Woolworths, Marks and Spencer, and British Home Stores. Other large chains tended to be far more specialist than today, such as WHSmith, which sold books and a little stationery, and Boots the Chemist, which sold toiletries and medicines. In a sign of what was to come, Britain's first

◄ A shopper places in her basket one person's weekly portion of rationed foods, 1951.

▲ Veteran footballer Horatio 'Raich' Carter serving in a typical confectioners and tobacconist shop, 1951.

◄ The interior of a grocer's shop, with all the wares on display, 1951.

supermarket opened in Streatham in 1951; the first Waitrose supermarket came four years later.

There was takeaway food in the 50s, but this was almost exclusively fish and chips; anything else was a rarity. Eating out was infrequent, so restaurants were also rare. Cafes on the other hand were commonplace; after the daily tour of the shops, a cup of coffee or tea was most welcome. Coffee bars and milk bars were the latest variations. Italian coffee bars, which made real coffee in noisy espresso machines, were a novelty; they also offered Italian rarebit, as pizza was then known. A great treat for children was a visit to the ice-cream parlour, again often Italian concerns, where you could have a cone or wafer, a sundae or milkshake.

At the start of the 50s hamburgers were only seen in US films, or cartoons such as *Popeye*, which included the character Wimpy who chomped his way through vast numbers of them. In 1954 the first Wimpy Bar was set up in the

Lyons Corner House in Coventry Street, London. These bars were a fast-food section inside Corner Houses, but they proved so successful that Wimpy restaurants began to be set up.

▲ A typical Lyons Nippy serving in a Corner House, 1952.

Relationships

▲ Teenagers rock and roll at the Palais de Dance in Nottingham, 1957, during a special lunch-hour session.

Attitudes towards young couples going out, or 'courting', were conservative. The war, with its uncertainties for the future, had created a live-for-today philosophy, but with peace, formality had returned. Daughters were kept on tight reins; prospective boyfriends would have to meet and be approved by parents before any dating could take place.

Meeting partners was difficult in these circumstances; many couples first met at school. Other likely places included youth centres, dances and the workplace. Clubs and societies, such as church groups, amateur dramatics, choirs, rambling and cycling clubs, were also good places to meet partners.

Gender roles were very clear. The man was expected to pay for the date. If eating out was involved, he would also be expected to take his companion's coat, hold her seat out while she sat down, and order for her. At the end of the date he would see his companion home, but a kiss goodnight on the first date was thought of as very forward, and was reserved for those 'going steady'.

Sex before marriage was very much frowned upon, so courting was encouraged to take place in public places, like cinemas or dances, with strict time limits set – home by 10.30 p.m. or else! In spite of this accidents occurred, and a quick marriage often followed; during the 50s, around 50,000 brides each year were already pregnant

on their wedding day, although there were still 35,000 illegitimate births annually.

If all went well it was still the norm to ask the girl's father for permission to marry. Marriage rates remained fairly constant throughout the decade, averaging around 350,000 a year. But there was a distinct gender imbalance which reduced people's chances of getting married, there being a significantly higher number of women than men. Over the decade, a man stood a two-thirds chance of getting married; with women it was only a half.

The Marriage Act of 1949 had come into effect in January 1950. Amazingly, the biggest change it introduced was to limit the minimum age for marriage in England and Wales to 16. It also extended the permissible times for marriage from 9 a.m. to 3 p.m. to 8 a.m. to 6 p.m., allowing people to even get married before work.

A shortage of housing, exacerbated by the Blitz, meant that most couples began married life living in a relative's spare room, usually of one or other of their parents, and spending a year, often more, saving up until a bedsit or flat became available. Living so close to the in-laws tested many a relationship; however, divorces fell from 31,000 in 1950 to 24,000 in 1959. Part of this was down to the high number of divorces among those who had married hastily at the beginning of the Second World War and then found that they were unsuited, or that one or both had changed over the years of separation caused by the war.

In 1950 there were 700,000 children born, dropping to 670,000 in 1955 and climbing to 750,000 by the end of the decade.

◀ A couple look at houses in the window of an estate agent, 1950.

Childhood

In February 1951 sweets came off ration after almost nine years, but the authorities had underestimated the response. Sweet shops were besieged by hordes of children and stocks were soon exhausted. The Government had no choice but to put sweets back on ration for two years, but on February 1953 they came off ration for good. In a more innocent time sweets included chocolate cigars, sweet cigarettes, and sweet tobacco made from desiccated coconut.

There were the normal toys: dolls, skipping ropes, plastic toy soldiers, cap guns, spud guns, yo-yos, roller skates and scooters being among the most popular. In 1958 there was a hula hoop craze, and in the same year Lego bricks first appeared in their familiar form.

▲ At the height of the hula hoop craze, 1958.

The highlight of most weeks for children was the Saturday Morning Pictures. This was a special show for children, costing 6d downstairs or 9d upstairs. Those upstairs had the advantage of being able to throw peanut shells, orange peel and other rubbish on to the kids below. The show consisted of short films, cartoons, a cliff-hanging serial such as *Flash Gordon*, and an adventure film, usually about a cowboy, during which the house would erupt in cheers for the 'goodies' and boos, hisses and cat-calls for the 'baddies'. In addition, there would be talent shows, fancy-dress competitions and sing-songs, including the club song. For ABC cinemas this was 'We are the Minors ABC', while Gaumont British kids sang, 'We come along, on Saturday morning, greeting everybody with a smile.'

On the wireless there was 'Children's Hour', including Larry the Lamb and Toytown. But there

◀ With eyes popping and mouths watering, these three youngsters gaze at the good things in store – for they can now buy sweets without points, 1953.

For younger children, Andy Pandy first appeared on television in July 1950, joined in December 1952 by Bill and Ben. Other 'Children's Hour' favourites included Rag, Tag and Bobtail from September 1953, The Woodentops, Crackerjack two years later, and in 1957 Pinky and Perky, the singing pig puppets.

In school, pupils would sit the eleven-plus exam at age 11, which would decide who went to the grammar gchool. In September 1957 education became much more fun, as BBC television for schools began.

were also serials in the evening, such as 'Dick Barton – Special Agent'; at its peak it had over 20 million listeners.

One of the most popular television programmes was *The Lone Ranger*, which ran from 1949 to 1957, starring Clayton Moore, with Jay Silverheels as his faithful sidekick Tonto. The show would start with its stirring theme tune, 'The William Tell Overture', and the Lone Ranger would climb onto his horse with the cry 'Hi-Yo, Silver! Away!', before thundering off into the distance. Other cowboy stars included William Boyd, who played Hopalong Cassidy, and Roy Rogers.

There were also adventure programmes such as *Robin Hood* in 1955, followed by *The Adventures of Sir Lancelot*, *The Adventures of William Tell*, *The Buccaneers*, *The Count of Monte Cristo*, and *Sword of Freedom*. In 1958 came *Blue Peter*, with presenters Christopher Trace and Leila Williams.

▲ Roy Rogers is shown with Dale Evans in this July 1952 photo.

Teenagers

The 50s saw the emergence of a new social group – teenagers. Previously, children had begun to be young grown-ups at 12, becoming full adults in stages up to the age of 21.

By the mid-1950s, 80 per cent of the five million British teenagers were working, earning good wages. Much of this was disposable income, spent on clothes, records and going out. Chief venues were the dancehall, cinema, and the coffee bar, where you could drink 'frothy coffee' and listen to the latest discs on the jukebox. Pubs were unpopular among the young as they tended to be very old fashioned and drab. Women, especially single women, were unwelcome, if not banned, and all-male company was not what the average teenage boy wanted.

Teens wanted their own fashions and the industry was happy to accommodate them. Fashion was often linked to the various styles of popular music, including jazz, skiffle, and rock and roll. Jazz was favoured by students and beatniks. The former went for casual dress: duffel coats and sloppy joe jumpers. Beatniks went more for black slacks and polo-necks, Abraham Lincoln-style beards for the boys, and heavy eye make-up and dark lipstick for the girls. Skiffle fans were influenced by the American folk scene: checked lumberjack shirts, turned-up jeans for the boys, flared dirndle skirts, or jumpers and tight trousers, particularly mid-calf-length pedal pushers, with flat shoes for the girls. Circular skirts bulked out by can-can petticoats, made of the new drip-dry nylon, were so called because they gave a flash of suspenders when the wearer spun round.

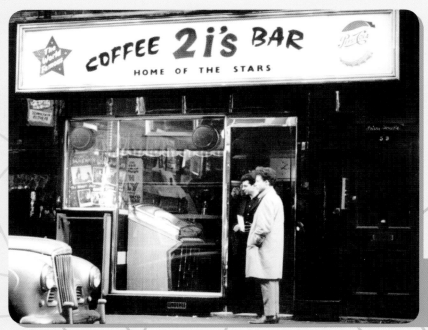

◄ A coffee bar in Old Compton Street, Soho, London, 1955.

Pete Murray (left), Freddie Mills and Josephine Douglas in 'Teddy boy' clothes for the BBC TV programme *Six-Five Special*, 1957.

boys'. They wore long, bright-coloured 'drape' jackets with velvet collars and flap pockets, tight 'drainpipe' trousers, a narrow 'slim-jim' tie and 'brothel creepers' – thick, crepe-soled shoes. Most important of all was the D.A. (duck's arse) haircut, with its accentuated quiff, achieved with lots of Brylcreme or similar hair dressing.

The Teds, as they were often known, soon gained a reputation for being troublemakers; slashing seats in cinemas was the most common charge against them, or fighting with such implements as knuckledusters, flick knives and bicycle chains. However, at 17 years old this was brought to a halt. National Service, which involved 18 months (or two years after October 1950) of compulsory military service, applied to all healthy males between the ages of 17 and 21 years. The only exemptions were those working in coal mining, farming or the merchant navy, and, interestingly, conscientious objectors. National Service began to be phased out from 1957.

One of the greatest influences on the teenage scene was the cinema, by now dominated by America. Several films had a huge impact on the direction of Britain's youth movement. The first of these was *The Wild One* (1953), starring Marlon Brando, which showed a leather-and-denim-clad motorcycle gang terrorising a small town. The fashion took off.

That year, Teddy boys evolved as a male fashion in London's East End – a nationalistic reaction to the invasion of American fashions. Their clothes were a revival of the Edwardian look, thus 'Teddy

A debutante reveals lace-trimmed bloomers as she whirls in a rock and roll dance number at the Star Chamber in London, 1957.

Health

In 1948 the National Health Service was born, available to all and financed entirely from taxation. Millions no longer had to ask themselves, 'Can we afford the doctor?' and were able to take full advantage of free prescriptions, dental care and glasses. The cost was huge, and in 1952 prescription charges of a shilling were introduced, as well as a flat rate of £1 for dental treatment.

Smog, or 'pea-soupers', was the curse of cities. Fog was added to by the smoke from millions of coal fires, forming a dense, smelly and dangerously toxic smoke screen. One of the worst was the Great Smog of London in 1952, which claimed 4,000 lives in four days, with twice as many dying from its effects soon after. This led to the 1956 Clean Air Act, which set up smokeless zones where it was illegal to burn coal. Only smokeless fuels, such as coke, could be used. This proved remarkably effective and the pea-souper became a thing of the past.

In 1954 Sir Richard Doll and Sir Austin Bradford Hill published a study in the *British Medical Journal* which stated that smokers were far more likely than non-smokers to die of lung cancer. This was ground-breaking; smoking was widespread and was often seen as good for you, touted as a stress-reducer.

Hospital stays are often confusing and distressing for children, but they were far more so in the early 1950s when parents were usually only allowed to visit offspring for an hour on Saturdays and Sundays. Worse still, there were rarely children's wards, so they were in mixed wards with adults, making a hospital stay boring, unpleasant and even traumatic. Great Ormond Street hospital worked hard to change the situation. The value of their work was recognised

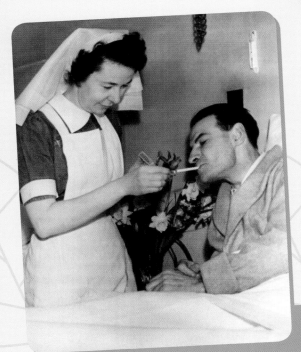

◄ A nurse lights a cigarette for a patient as he lies in bed at Bangor Hospital, County Down, Northern Ireland, 1953.

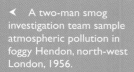

◄ A two-man smog investigation team sample atmospheric pollution in foggy Hendon, north-west London, 1956.

▼ A nurse shows a young mother confined to an iron lung her newly born son. She is paralysed from polio, 1959.

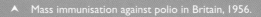

▲ Mass immunisation against polio in Britain, 1956.

Poliomyelitis, often called polio or 'infantile paralysis', is a disease that causes spinal and respiratory paralysis and can lead to death. In the 1950s there were 45,000 cases in the UK; hundreds died and even more were left wearing calipers on their legs, or condemned to long periods in an 'iron lung'. The disease struck fear into the popular imagination and during the early years of the decade work was carried out to develop a vaccine. In 1958 a widespread vaccination programme was rolled out in the UK, drastically cutting the number of cases.

Tuberculosis, otherwise known as TB or 'consumption', was another horrific illness, and although a vaccine had been produced in the 1920s, there was a great deal of public mistrust. However, in 1953 the UK introduced universal BCG immunisation, mainly through the schools. That year, in another leap forward, DNA was discovered.

and from 1954 daily visits for children began to be introduced in many hospitals.

Diphtheria, a highly contagious bacterial infection, had at one time been a real problem. In 1940 there had been over 46,000 cases, resulting in 2,500 deaths. However, a vaccine was introduced to the UK in 1941, and by 1957 the number of cases had plummeted to just 37 cases and six deaths.

Fashion

As the decade started, men's clothes were still very much as they had been for the previous 20 years. A basic outfit consisted of the three-piece lounge suit or country suit, shirt and tie, lace-up leather shoes and, for outdoors, a trilby hat or flat cap, with a knee-length macintosh or heavy overcoat.

Suits and ties were worn for all but the most informal of occasions; among the middle and upper classes it was still the norm to dress for dinner. For less formal occasions, the three-piece suit might give way to a jacket or blazer, flannels and a sleeveless jumper, normally with a tie. On holiday, or for golf, for example, the jacket might be replaced by a long-sleeved pullover, or in hot weather a short-sleeved shirt and slipover, worn tieless and open-necked with the collar outside the jumper.

Women were far more open to change. The progression from small local seamstresses and workshops to mass production brought about by the war remained, bringing the cost of ready-made clothing down dramatically. Most women could now afford a fashionable outfit once or twice a year, especially as Utility clothing, designed to be well-made but cheap due to subsidies and its purchase tax-free state, continued to be produced until 1952.

The basic outfit was the dress or suit, around knee-length, and, following Dior's New Look of 1947, flared from a tight waist. For housework, an apron or 'pinny' would be worn over the dress. As with men, hats were a must outdoors, as were gloves for more formal occasions: lace or cotton in summer; wool, fur or leather in winter.

Children's clothes were, to a great extent, junior versions of their parents'. Boys wore shirt, tie and slipover with short trousers up to the age of 12, and thereafter long versions. Girls wore dresses with cardigans. Sandals were normal summer wear, with

▲ Men's Fashion Parade at the Royal Festival Hall. A double-breasted lounge suit and bowler hat, 1955.

▲ Queen Elizabeth II following the wedding of her cousin, at St George's Chapel, Windsor, 1957.

boots or shoes worn in the winter, with long socks or short bobby socks, for both boys and girls.

For women who followed the fashions closely, 1950 saw the appearance of the sheath dress – which was, as the name suggests, tight-fitting – and the trumpet coat, which clung down to the knees and then flared to a mid-calf-length hemline. This was soon followed by the trumpet skirt. In 1953 the first stiletto heels arrived in Britain – floors up and down the country would never be the same. Other fashion styles would include the H-line in 1954, followed one year later by the A-line and the tube dress. The year 1957 saw the sack dress and the spindle line, followed a year later by the trapeze dress.

For men, new fashions tended to be muted forms of teenage styles. One fashion was the Italian suit: lightweight, single-breasted and long. With narrow lapels and tight trousers, it had undertones of the Teddy boys' drape. To match this slim look, ties became 'slim jims' and shoes became more pointed (like the winklepicker) or chunky (like the 'brothel creeper'). Suede shoes also became acceptable.

▼ A tailored dress of woollen tweed in what has been named Gregoriana style, 1959.

Popular Culture

The wireless, as radio was almost universally known, was, at the start of the 1950s, overwhelmingly the most popular form of home entertainment. A favourite show was 'Mrs Dale's Diary', first broadcast in January 1948 and running until 1969. It began with harp music and Mrs Dale, acting as a narrator, reading from her diary, with immortal lines such as 'I'm worried about Jim' (her husband, Dr Dale), before going into the full cast.

In May 1950 'The Archers' began to be broadcast by the Midlands Home Service every weekday. The programme was intended to be a way of giving farmers and smallholders information to help improve productivity at a time when food was still rationed. It was, however, remarkably well received as a drama and the BBC decided to go national in 1951.

Television broadcasting had begun in the mid-1930s. By the early 50s a TV was still something of a rarity. In black and white, and with a single channel – the BBC – it was often uninspiring. Then in 1954 the Television Act was passed, which was intended to break the BBC's monopoly.

The first six commercial franchises were awarded for London, the Midlands and the North of England (two for each – one for weekdays and one for weekends). London's Associated-Rediffusion station opened on

22 September 1955, followed by the Midlands the following February and the North in May.

The Grove Family, a BBC series broadcast from 1954 and 1957, is usually regarded as British television's first soap opera, but *Emergency Ward 10*, which was, as its title suggests, a hospital drama, was a far bigger hit. ITV began broadcasting it in 1957, continuing for a decade.

Popular music in the early 1950s consisted mainly of ballads; number ones in the hit parade included 'I Believe' by Frankie Laine, 'Three Coins in a Fountain' by Frank Sinatra, and 'Secret Love' by Doris Day. Other stars included Perry Como, Johnnie Ray and Tony Bennett. British number one artists included Jimmy Young, Dickie Valentine and Alma Cogan. Instrumentals were popular too, including 'Oh, Mein Papa' by Eddie Calvert, 'Let's

◄ The luxury television set in action, 1951.

> Singer Cliff Richard on stage, 1959.

◄ A farmer listens to the radio while milking a cow in December 1951.

Have Another Party' by Winifred Atwell, and 'Song from Moulin Rouge' by Mantovani.

Then came July 1955 and 'Rock Around the Clock' by Bill Hayley. It was the biggest selling record of the decade, with 1.3 million copies sold. From that point on the hit records were almost all rock and roll numbers, including 'Diana' by Paul Anka, 'Jailhouse Rock' by Elvis Presley, and 'It Doesn't Matter Anymore' by Buddy Holly.

British rockers included Adam Faith, Cliff Richard & The Drifters (who later changed their name to The Shadows), Billy Fury, Marty Wilde and Joe Brown. Joe had been a guitarist in skiffle groups, skiffle being a particularly British form of music using instruments such as the tea-chest base and a washboard 'strummed' with a thimble-bedecked hand. It achieved a short-lived popularity in the mid-50s with stars such as Lonnie Donegan, but it was swept aside by the raw power of rock and roll.

▲ Singer and actor Frank Sinatra plays the piano, 1954.

Transport

The rapid growth of personal wealth during the 1950s was reflected in the increase in road traffic. With the end of petrol rationing in 1950 there were 2.3 million private and light goods vehicles licensed, rising to 3.9 million in 1955, and 5.7 million by 1960.

Many of the new cars were British-built. Popular models included the Morris Minor, which was first produced in 1948 as a two-door saloon; a four-door model appeared in 1950, followed by the Traveller (a wood-framed estate). The Morris Minor was reliable, if somewhat slow. In 1950 the 1098cc tourer had a top speed of about 60mph. However, with a fuel consumption of over 40mpg and a cost of under £400, it was an ideal low-income family car.

Other popular British cars included the Hillman Minx and, perhaps the most evocative of the era, the Vauxhall Cresta. With lots of chrome, rear fins and sweeping wings, the Cresta was the epitome of the jet-age style. The E version, produced in 1954, had a six-cylinder, 2262cc engine and came with such luxuries as a heater and cigar lighter as standard, plus a choice of leather or fabric upholstery, and optional two-tone paintwork and radio. With a top speed of over 80mph, it could accelerate from 0–60 in 20 seconds. However, the petrol consumption of less than 25mpg and a cost of over £900 were considerable drawbacks.

But fashions were changing; the old, huge American-style cars were becoming yesterday's

▲ Around 500 Morris Minors on the jetty of the Samuel Williams wharf of the London docks, destined for Canada, 1950.

◄ A Vauxhall Cresta at the London Motor Show, Earls Court, 1957.

The rise in car ownership and the building of better roads had an adverse effect on public transport. In 1952 the last London tram drove into New Cross depot to cheers from a huge crowd. Years of neglect had left British Rail with an ageing system, and in 1954 a modernisation plan was published. Proposals included the electrification of main lines, the large-scale introduction of diesel locomotives, and some closures. Sadly, many of the proposals were carried out badly, which had the effect of encouraging, rather than reversing, the move to the roads.

news. The new, youth-inspired fashion needed something small and fun. In August 1959 BMC introduced the two-door Mini jointly as the Austin Seven and the Morris Mini-Minor.

For those who could not afford a car, a motorcycle was a popular alternative. The 50s were the high point for British motorbikes, with popular makes including BSA, Triumph, Norton, Matchless and Royal Enfield.

All of this traffic needed bigger, faster roads; the first motorway, the Preston Bypass, opened in 1958, followed a year later by the first section of the M1 between Watford and Crick, near Rugby.

Air travel was becoming more affordable; in 1955 there were a million domestic passengers on UK airlines. The first jet airliner, the De Havilland Comet 1, entered service in 1952 on the London to Johannesburg route. By 1954 a series of crashes had caused the Comets to be grounded after metal fatigue was found. In 1958 the Comet 4 and the Boeing 707-120 were introduced, with the first transatlantic jet service beginning in October that year.

▲ The Eastern Region's express *The Elizabethan* leaving King's Cross Station to travel the 393 miles to Edinburgh in 6½ hours – the fastest ever non-stop journey between London and Edinburgh, 1954.

▲ A tram and bus at Victoria Embankment during the last week of London tramcars, 1952.

Famous Faces

◄ King George VI, Princess Elizabeth and Princess Margaret at the christening of Princess Anne, 1950.

► Racing driver Stirling Moss sitting in his Maserati after winning the Aintree 200 motor race, 1954.

On 15 August 1950 the second child of Princess Elizabeth and the Duke of Edinburgh, Princess Anne, was born at Clarence House. The following May, King George VI, a heavy smoker, had his left lung removed following the discovery of a malignant tumour. Nine months later, at the age of 56, he died from a coronary thrombosis and was buried at Windsor Castle. He was succeeded by his eldest daughter, Princess Elizabeth, who was crowned Queen Elizabeth II on 2 June 1953. The young, attractive queen summed up the feeling of the post-war period; hers would be the second Elizabethan age.

As if to confirm this idea, on the day of the coronation news reached London that Mount Everest had at last been conquered, by New Zealander Edmund Hilary and Sherpa Tenzing Norgay. Hilary and expedition leader John Hunt were knighted, while Tenzing received the George Medal.

The Queen's sister, Princess Margaret, caused controversy by falling in love with a married man, Group Captain Peter Townsend. In 1952 he divorced his first wife and a year later proposed to Margaret. Many in the establishment were against the union and the Church of England refused to marry them. The couple subsequently drifted apart. Margaret's nephew, Prince Charles, was created Prince of Wales in July 1958, although he was not invested as such until 1969.

The cult of the show business or sporting star as a celebrity was in full swing; of the latter, Stirling Moss, a British motor-racing champion, had 16 Formula One successes throughout the 50s. 'Fearless' Freddie Mills was a British boxer who became world light heavyweight champion in 1948. In January 1950 he lost his title to American Joey Maxim. In spite of this, Mills remained in the public eye, with cameo roles in films such as *Carry on Constable* and as a presenter on the TV programme *Six-Five Special*. He was also the owner of a Soho restaurant and nightclub, and was a friend of the Kray Twins. The Krays, Ronnie and Reggie, were professional East End boxers who were imprisoned after going absent without leave from National Service in 1952; they subsequently built up a huge criminal empire.

◄ Sardar Tenzing Norgay of Nepal and Edmund P. Hillary of New Zealand conquered Mount Everest, the world's highest peak, on 29 May 1953.

Another friend of the Krays was actress Diana Dors. Curvaceous, feisty and blonde, she was held up as the British Marilyn Monroe. Monroe herself had been signed by 20th Century Fox in 1946, but drew little attention until 1950. She then took on a succession of dumb blonde roles in films such as *Some Like it Hot*.

The French response was Brigitte Bardot, who rose to fame in 1957 in *And God Created Woman*, while Italy produced Sophia Loren who moved to Hollywood in 1957. It was the time of the statuesque film star as glamour icon, which peaked in April 1956 when Grace Kelly married Prince Rainier of Monaco.

Other British stars included comedians such as the Goons, Tony Hancock, Frankie Howerd, Tommy Cooper and Charlie Drake, and a rich vein of character actors, including Alec Guinness, Terry Thomas, Dora Bryan, Jimmy Edwards, Alastair Sim and Beryl Reid.

Politics

In February 1950 Labour under Clement Attlee were re-elected, but with a reduced majority of five. This led to another election in October 1951, this time won by the Conservatives with a majority of 17. Once again Winston Churchill became Prime Minister. He retired in April 1955, being replaced by Sir Anthony Eden, and in the General Election one month later the Conservatives were returned with a majority of 60.

In 1953, in the USA, Democratic President Harry S. Truman was replaced by Republican Dwight D. Eisenhower, who had been Supreme Allied Commander in the Second World War, and his vice-president, Richard Nixon.

In Russia that March Josef Stalin died, to be replaced by Georgy Malenkov. There followed a two-year power struggle between Malenkov and Nikita Khrushchev, which the latter won, becoming First Secretary in September 1955. Khrushchev denounced Stalinism, giving hope to countries seeking independence from the USSR.

In Hungary, in October 1956, a demonstration of thousands of people was fired upon by the State Security Police; violence rapidly escalated. At first the Politburo made conciliatory

↑ President Eisenhower with Prime Minister Macmillan in 1959.

noises, but then it moved to crush the revolt, with Soviet forces invading the country on 4 November. Hungarian radio pleaded for help from the West, but none came, and on 10 November resistance came to an end. While this tightened Soviet control over Eastern Europe, it destroyed any large-scale support for the Soviet system in the West.

In July 1956 Egyptian President Abdul Nasser nationalised the Suez Canal Company, which had been run by the French with Britain as the largest single shareholder. While technically legal, Britain and France saw the action as an insult to their prestige at a time when their positions as world powers were on the wane. They began to plan a military operation and, in October, the

◄ Winston Churchill makes a general election polling day tour of his constituency – Woodford, Essex, 1950.

▲ On 10 January 1957 Harold Macmillan becomes Prime Minister after Sir Anthony Eden resigns.

▼ Lt Colonel Gamal Abdel Nasser, the 36-year-old leader of the Revolutionary Command Council of Egypt, in 1954.

recently formed State of Israel agreed to strike against Egypt, capturing the Gaza Strip and the Sinai Peninsula. This allowed France and Britain to send in troops as 'peacekeepers' and bomb Egyptian positions.

However, Eisenhower was deeply concerned and refused to back France and Britain who were condemned at the UN. On 4 November the General Assembly overwhelmingly supported a proposal to send in a real UN peacekeeping force with no British or French involvement. Without US support, Britain and France had no option but to withdraw. Israel, too, withdrew from the Sinai Peninsula and the Gaza Strip. This was done by the end of the year and Eden resigned 'due to ill health' in January 1957, to be replaced by Harold Macmillan. Many saw this as the end of Britain as a major power.

In July Macmillan made a speech in which he declared that the British public had 'never had it so good'. By now, the long post-war years of austerity were past, and in October 1959 he led the Conservatives to another General Election victory, with a majority of 100. Also that year, Ghana, the Gold Coast and the Malayan states received their independence and became members of the Commonwealth, demonstrating that not all Britain's former colonies caused problems.

War & Peace

One of the flashpoints throughout the 50s was Cyprus, with its mixed Greek and Turkish population. In 1950 Archbishop Makarios, head of the Cypriot Orthodox Church, was elected the political and spiritual leader of the island. There were calls among the Greek Cypriots for *Enosis* – unification with Greece – and in April 1955 a series of bomb attacks marked the start of a guerrilla campaign for *Enosis* by the National Organisation of Cypriot Fighters (EOKA), led by George Grivas. In February 1959 the British Government agreed to grant Cyprus independence.

While the Cold War was unfolding in Europe, in Asia the same clash of ideologies produced real war. Previously, much of the continent had been controlled by European states, but Japanese forces had swept them aside, showing the frailty of these once-great empires. Nationalists and Communists, armed by the Allies, had harried the Japanese occupiers. With liberation, the former imperial masters had tried to return, but the mood had swung towards independence.

Korea had been part of the Japanese Empire, but in 1948 the UN recognised the Republic of Korea as the sole legal Government of Korea, a decision not acceptable to the eastern bloc.

▲ US Marines go aboard the Navy transport USS *Henrico*, 1950.

◄ British soldiers on guard near the barbed-wire barricade which divides the Greek and Turkish quarters of Nicosia, Cyprus, 1958.

◄ US Military Police guard North Korean soldiers, captured 4 September 1950.

the many Communist insurgencies of the period this turned into a full-scale war, which culminated in the battle of Dien Bien Phu in early 1954, where the French army was soundly beaten. The war ended shortly afterwards and France agreed to withdraw forces from all its former colonies in what was known as French Indochina. Vietnam was divided at the 17th parallel, the north being controlled by the Communist Viet Minh, under its leader Ho Chi Minh, and the south under Emperor Bao Dai.

The world was splitting along ideological lines. In May 1955 a similar mutual defence treaty was signed in Warsaw, known as the Warsaw Pact. Signatories were Albania, Bulgaria, Czechoslovakia, East Germany, Hungary, Poland, Romania and the Soviet Union.

The country consequently divided between the Communist north and the West-leaning south. In June 1950 the Korean War broke out when North Korea, supported by the People's Republic of China and the Soviet Union, invaded the south, which was backed by the United Nations, including Britain. After a bloody and indecisive war which left 5 million dead, and with the threat of nuclear weapons always lurking, the USA, North Korea and China signed an armistice in July 1953, bringing open conflict to an end. The tension, nevertheless, would remain.

NATO, the North Atlantic Treaty Organization, had been set up in 1949. Its aim, according to Lord Ismay, its first Secretary General, was 'to keep the Russians out, the Americans in, and the Germans down'. The Korean War, with its alliance of Russia, China and North Korea, added impetus to NATO, and countries such as Greece and Turkey joined in 1952, followed by West Germany in 1955.

Vietnam had been under French control, but when they tried to return after the Second World War they were met with resistance from the Vietnamese, who wanted independence. Unlike

➤ Ho Chi Minh, president of communist North Vietnam, in 1957.

The Festival of Britain was held in the summer of 1951 to promote the British contribution to science, technology, industrial design, architecture and the arts. Events were held in places including Glasgow, Cardiff, Stratford-upon-Avon, York, Bath and Oxford. The centrepiece was on London's South Bank where concerts were held at the newly opened Royal Festival Hall, the first ones being conducted by Sir Malcolm Sargent and Sir Adrian Boult. On a different note, the first Miss World Beauty Pageant took place, billed as the 'Festival Bikini Contest'.

One of the highlights was the Skylon, a cigar-shaped aluminium-clad tower supported by cables. The base of the tower was nearly 50 feet above the ground, and its top almost 300 feet high, and it was lit from within at night. Sadly, the Skylon was scrapped in 1952 on the orders of Winston Churchill, who viewed the whole festival as propaganda for Attlee's Labour Government.

Another part of the South Bank Exhibition was the Dome of Discovery, containing exhibits on

the Land, the Earth, Polar, the Sea, the Sky, Outer Space, the Physical World, and the Living World. Almost 8.5 million people visited the South Bank during the festival.

In November 1952 Agatha Christie's play 'The Mousetrap' started its run at the New Ambassadors Theatre in London; it became the longest-running show in the world, and at the time of writing is still going!

In January 1953 there was the Great Flood, as it became known. A huge storm crossed between the Orkney and Shetland Isles, then down the east coast. Over 1,000 miles of coastline was

◄ The new Skylon tower at the Festival of Britain, London, 1951.

> Flooding in King's Lynn, Norfolk, 1953.

◄ A view of the Festival of Britain, showing the Dome of Discovery, Skylon tower and Royal Festival Hall, 1951.

After the Second World War, Oswald Mosley's British Union of Fascists (BUF) had re-emerged, chiefly as a reaction to immigration. Teddy boys in London's East End began to be hostile towards black families in the area, and during the summer of 1958 there was an increase in violent attacks. At the end of August a mob of 300–400, including many Teds, attacked the houses of West Indian residents in London's Notting Hill. Riots and incursions went on every night until 5 September, during the course of which 140 people were arrested. Subsequently, 72 white and 36 black people were charged.

battered and 400 square miles flooded. Twenty-four thousand properties were seriously damaged and 30,000 people had to be evacuated from their homes. The death toll was 307, including 19 in Scotland, 38 in Felixstowe, 58 in Canvey Island and 37 in Jaywick. A further 224 were lost at sea.

On 13 July 1955 Ruth Ellis became the last woman to be hanged in Britain. She was accused of shooting her lover, racing driver David Blakely. She immediately admitted it and was sentenced to death. There was a great deal of public sympathy for what was clearly a crime of passion; a petition signed by 50,000 people was presented to the Home Secretary but he refused clemency. The revulsion many felt added to the calls for the abolition of the death penalty.

▲ A race riot in Notting Hill, London, 31 August 1958.

◄ The signing of the treaty establishing the European Economic Community in 1957.

▼ The booking photograph of Rosa Parks, 1956.

After a second great European war, many wanted the continent to be more unified. In 1951 the Treaty of Paris was signed, creating the European Coal and Steel Community, comprising of Belgium, France, Italy, Luxembourg, the Netherlands and West Germany. This was followed by the Treaty of Rome of 1957. This created the European Economic Community (EEC), also known as the Common Market, from the original six countries.

The first hydrogen bomb was tested by the USA in the Marshall Islands in November 1952. The development of ever-more powerful weapons worried many, leading to the formation of the Campaign for Nuclear Disarmament, or CND, which was launched in February 1958. That Easter the first Aldermaston March took place in Britain.

In South Africa in 1952, under what was known as the Pass Laws Act, it became compulsory for all black South Africans over the age of 16 to carry a 'pass book' with them at all times when in white areas. This contained fingerprints, photographs and details of employment. Anyone without such a pass would face arrest and imprisonment. Two years later, the US Supreme Court declared segregation to be illegal in the US, following the case of Brown v. Board of Education. While the case concerned segregation in education, the decision had deep implications. Being declared illegal did not mean segregation was abolished, however, and many states chose to ignore the ruling.

In December 1955 Rosa Parks, an African American woman, boarded a bus in Montgomery and sat just behind the seats reserved for whites. These became filled and when a white man got on, the driver told the blacks sitting behind the white section to give up their seats. Mrs Parks quietly refused, was arrested and convicted of violating the segregation laws. Local civil rights activists began a boycott of the Montgomery bus system. They chose a young Baptist minister, Martin Luther King Jr, as their leader. The boycott lasted over a year until the Supreme Court ruled the law unconstitutional and the buses were integrated.

In October 1957 the Soviet Union launched Sputnik. The first artificial satellite, Sputnik was less than 2 feet in diameter and weighed under 220 pounds. The following year, in America, President Eisenhower set up the National Aeronautics and Space Administration (NASA) to look at peaceful applications in space science. One year later the Soviet Union scored another first when Laika the dog became the first creature to orbit the Earth in November 1957. Unfortunately she died a few hours into the mission. The USSR continued to lead the space race when, in September 1959, Luna 2 became the first manmade object to reach the Moon.

In China, in 1958, Mao Tse-tung launched the Great Leap Forward. This campaign aimed to transform the country through industrialisation and collectivisation, under which private farming was prohibited. The great upheaval in food production led to what became known as the Great Chinese Famine, in which at least 18 million died.

In 1959 the US-backed president of Cuba, Batista, was overthrown by Communist revolutionaries, and Fidel Castro became Prime Minister.

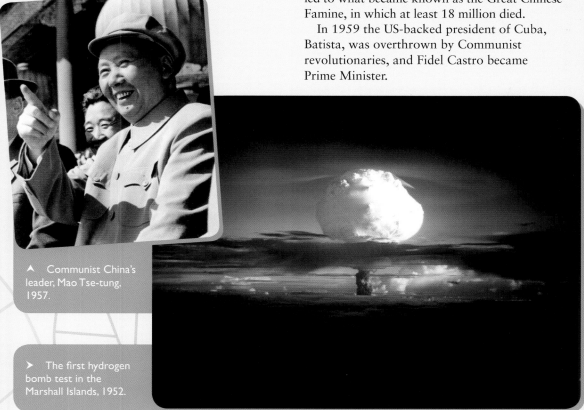

▲ Communist China's leader, Mao Tse-tung, 1957.

➤ The first hydrogen bomb test in the Marshall Islands, 1952.

Important Dates

1950

In June the BBC broadcast the pilot episode of 'The Archers'.

1951

In May the King opens the Festival of Britain, featuring the Skylon, the Royal Festival Hall and the Dome of Discovery.

1952

In February King George VI dies from lung cancer and Princess Elizabeth becomes Queen in what is hailed as the 'new Elizabethan age'.

1953

In June, on the very day of Queen Elizabeth's coronation, news is received that Hilary and Tensing have reached the top of Mount Everest.

1954

In July meat and bacon go 'off-ration'; food rationing is ended after 14 years.

1955

The first independent television channels begin broadcasting, bringing to an end the BBC's monopoly.

1956

In late 1956 comes the Suez crisis; British and French troops seize control of the canal but are soon forced to withdraw in the face of international pressure.

1957

Prime Minister Harold Macmillan, 'SuperMac', tells supporters that 'most of our people have never had it so good'.

1958

In February the plane carrying the Manchester United team, 'Busby's Babes', crashes on take-off at Munich; eight players are among the 23 killed.

1959

Britain's first motorway, the M1, is opened between Watford and Crick.

Acknowledgements

Written by Mike Brown. The author has asserted his moral rights.
Edited by Abbie Wood.
Designed by Jemma Cox.

All photographs have been supplied by PA Images.

Every effort has been made to contact the copyright holders; the publisher will be pleased to rectify any omissions in future editions.

Text © Pitkin Publishing.

Publication in this form © Pitkin Publishing 2014.

Printed in Great Britain.

ISBN 978-1-84165-539-0   1/14